# The Year in History
# 1942

Whitman Publishing, LLC

www.whitman.com

© 2012 Whitman Publishing, LLC
3101 Clairmont Rd., Suite G, Atlanta GA 30329

All rights reserved, including duplication of any kind or storage in electronic or visual retrieval systems. Permission is granted for writers to use a limited number of brief excerpts and quotations in printed reviews and magazine articles provided credit is given to the title of the work and the publisher. Written permission is required for other uses, including in books, any use of illustrations, and any use of any information or illustrations in electronic or other media.

Correspondence concerning this book may be directed to the publisher at the address above, attention: The Year in History: 1942.

ISBN: 0794837085
Printed in China

Scan the QR code at left or visit us at www.whitman.com for a complete listing of collectibles-related books, supplies, and storage products.

Whitman®

# Contents

**Introduction** — 4

**Chapter 1**
Famous People Born in 1942 — 6

**Chapter 2**
The Cost of Living in 1942 — 16

**Chapter 3**
Day-by-Day Calendar of 1942 — 22

**Chapter 4**
Pop Culture in 1942 — 112

Credits and Acknowledgments — 120

# Introduction

The year was 1942, and America was finally in the war.

Of course, some would argue that America had been in for quite some time; at the very least, the United States could hardly have been said to be neutral with regard to the conflagration that was sweeping across Europe and the Far East. Nevertheless, there was still stiff resistance to the idea of American involvement in another European war. Even after the devastating sneak attack on Pearl Harbor—which left more than 2,400 dead—and the subsequent declaration of war on Imperial Japan, war with Germany was still a tough sell. The fact that Germany declared war on us a few days later made it go down a little easier, though, and one of the outcomes of the First Washington Conference was an agreement between President Roosevelt and British prime minister Winston Churchill that the defeat of the Nazi war machine was the first objective of the Allied forces. Churchill had spent that anxious Christmas of 1941 at the White House, conferring—and commiserating—with FDR over the war, and laying the groundwork for a unified military strategy between the Allied powers. The two also laid out a blueprint for future world peace and convinced 24 other nations to sign on to the dream as well. These United Nations, as they christened the organization on January 1, 1942, would, they hoped, ensure that such a horrific conflict between nations would never erupt again.

The year 1942 would, of course, prove to be filled with anxiety as citizens mobilized for the war effort, but it also brought forth the kind of determination and resolve that exemplified the American spirit. Production lines that had previously turned out cars and other manufactured goods were quickly adapted to the production of tanks, jeeps, weapons, and airplanes. As the male workforce put down their tools and picked up rifles instead, women by the thousands stepped into those jobs and kept production at an all-time high; thanks to them, the awesome manufacturing power of U.S. industry managed a 250 percent rise in output by August of 1942. And we were just getting started.

Meanwhile, the war made itself felt in day-to-day life in ways both small and large. Patriotism and sacrifice became the theme for 1942—not just how best to fight the enemy abroad, but how those on the home front could best support those troops and ensure their speedy return. Wartime posters urged Americans above all to be careful—to watch what they said, lest choice information fall on enemy ears; to employ safety in the factories, lest a workplace injury stem the flow of production; and to waste not a single precious drop of fuel through unnecessary travel. The government asked that everyone contribute to the war effort, by raising money through war bonds or salvaging scrap metal and cooking fat that could be recycled into essential war matériel, but mostly by simply doing without, so that the armed forces could have more food and equipment on the front lines.

In fact, as the government all but put a halt to nonessential production, conservation and even rationing became the norm. Families were encouraged to grow their own fruits and vegetables in "victory gardens," and the public responded, planting everywhere a free patch of land could be found: backyards, empty neighborhood lots, even rooftops in the heart of the city. In all, an estimated 20 million victory gardens were started, and by the end of the war these small plots had produced some ten million tons of fresh fruits and vegetables.

Even events as trivial as football games would be affected by wartime anxiety and caution: with Pearl Harbor still fresh in the public consciousness, for instance, the government prohibited all large gatherings on the West Coast for the duration of the war. And so the Rose Bowl, usually played in the stadium at Pasadena, was played instead on the other side of the country at Duke University in Durham, North Carolina. (The home field advantage proved no benefit for Duke; the Blue Devils lost to the Oregon State Beavers 20–16.)

Born on January 14, 1942, Cassius Clay would grow up to be Muhammad Ali—one of the most charismatic heavyweight boxing champions of all time.

# Famous People Born in 1942

"When I was born in 1942, World War II was still going," said Graham Nash (born February 2), of the legendary folk-rock band Crosby, Stills, Nash & Young. "And I began to realize when I became a young adult that if we don't teach our kids a better way of relating to their fellow human beings, the very future of humanity on the planet is in jeopardy." It can be seen from his extensive charity work that Mr. Nash suited action to his words, but then again, so many of the remarkable individuals born in 1942 might have expressed similar sentiments, if asked. Indeed, few can be said to have contributed as much to the advancement of knowledge and of the human race in general as has Professor Stephen Hawking (January 8), but 1942 would yield champions in every field of human endeavor, from sports heroes like Muhammad Ali (January 17) to beloved entertainers like Barbra Streisand (April 24) and Aretha Franklin (March 25); pop-culture figures like Harrison Ford (July 14) and Broadway superstar Michael Crawford (January 19); and transformational figures like civil rights icon Charlayne Hunter-Gault (February 27) and children's advocate and author Andrew Vachss (October 19). Not only did they change the world in their own right, but they inspired others to change the world as well. Who can argue the profound effect of cultural icons like Jimi Hendrix (November 27) or Paul McCartney (June 18), or dispute the impact that Isaac Hayes's (August 20) unforgettable theme had alongside Richard Roundtree's (September 7) explosive performance as hardboiled 1970s urban detective Shaft? The world they were born into may have been a tumultuous one, but the children of 1942 have certainly more than done their part to make it better—and far more interesting.

Martin Scorsese, born on November 17, would become a highly successful and influential movie director.

# Famous People Born in 1942

**January 1**—Country Joe McDonald, musician (Country Joe and the Fish)
**January 1**—Don Novello, a.k.a. Father Guido Sarducci, comedian *(Saturday Night Live)*
**January 5**—Charlie Rose, journalist and talk show host *(CBS Night Watch)*
**January 5**—Cliff Potts, actor *(Silent Running)*
**January 8**—Stephen Hawking, English theoretical physicist and author *(A Brief History of Time)*
**January 8**—Yvette Mimieux, actress *(The Time Machine, The Black Hole)*
**January 9**—K Callan, actress *(Lois and Clark: The New Adventures of Superman)*
**January 10**—Jim Croce, singer and songwriter ("Bad, Bad Leroy Brown")
**January 10**—Walter Hill, director *(The Warriors, 48 Hours)*
**January 11**—Clarence Clemons, musician (Bruce Springsteen's E Street Band) and actor
**January 12**—Bernardine Dohrn, 1960s radical, former leader of Weather Underground
**January 14**—Dave "Soup" Campbell, baseball player and sportscaster (Detroit Lions)
**January 15**—Edward "Sonny" Bivins, singer (The Manhattans)
**January 16**—Barbara Lynn, blues guitarist and singer ("You'll Lose a Good Thing")
**January 16**—Billy Francis, musician (Dr. Hook and the Medicine Show)
**January 17**—Muhammad Ali (born Cassius Clay), heavyweight championship boxer
**January 17**—Randy Boone, actor *(Cimarron Strip, The Virginian)*
**January 17**—Nancy Parsons, actress *(Porky's)*
**January 19**—Michael Crawford, Broadway star *(Phantom of the Opera)*
**January 19**—Shelly Fabares, actress and singer *(The Donna Reed Show, Coach)*
**January 21**—Mac Davis, singer ("Baby, Don't Get Hooked on Me"), songwriter, and actor
**January 24**—Gary Hart, professional wrestler and manager
**January 25**—Carl Eller, pro football Hall of Famer (Minnesota Vikings)
**January 27**—James Cromwell, actor *(L.A. Confidential, Babe)*
**January 27**—John Witherspoon, actor and comedian *(Friday)*
**January 29**—Katharine Ross, actress *(The Graduate, Butch Cassidy and the Sundance Kid)*
**January 30**—Marty Balin, singer (Jefferson Airplane / Jefferson Starship)
**February 1**—Terry Jones, Welsh comedian (Monty Python)
**February 2**—Bo Hopkins, actor *(The Wild Bunch)*
**February 2**—Graham Nash, English musician (Crosby, Stills, Nash & Young; The Hollies)

Born on March 25, Aretha Franklin would grow up to become the Queen of Soul.

# Famous People Born in 1942

**February 5**—Roger Staubach, Heisman Trophy winner and NFL Hall of Famer (Dallas Cowboys)
**February 6**—James Loewen, sociologist and historian *(Lies My Teacher Told Me)*
**February 8**—Fritz Peterson, baseball player (New York Yankees)
**February 8**—Robert Klein, comedian and actor *(Hooper)*
**February 9**—Carole King, singer and songwriter *(Tapestry)*
**February 10**—Jimmy Merchant, singer (Frankie Lymon and the Teenagers)
**February 11**—Otis Clay, gospel/R&B singer ("That's How It Is")
**February 12**—Pat Dobson, baseball player (Baltimore Orioles)
**February 13**—Carol Lynley, actress *(The Night Stalker, The Poseidon Adventure)*
**February 13**—Peter Tork, musician and actor (The Monkees)
**February 20**—Peter Strauss, actor *(Rich Man, Poor Man)*
**February 20**—Phil Esposito, Canadian hockey player (Boston Bruins, New York Rangers)
**February 24**—Joe Lieberman, U.S. senator (I-Connecticut)
**February 24**—Paul Jones, English musician (Manfred Mann)
**February 25**—Karen Grassle, actress *(Little House on the Prairie)*
**February 27**—Charlayne Hunter-Gault, civil rights figure and journalist *(In My Place)*
**February 27**—Robert H. Grubbs, winner of the 2005 Nobel Prize in chemistry
**February 28**—Frank Bonner, actor *(WKRP in Cincinnati)*
**February 28**—Brian Jones, English musician (The Rolling Stones)
**March 2**—John Irving, author *(The Cider House Rules)*
**March 2**—Lou Reed, musician (The Velvet Underground)
**March 6**—Ben Murphy, actor *(Alias Smith and Jones)*
**March 7**—Michael Eisner, CEO of the Walt Disney Company (1984–2005)
**March 7**—Tammy Faye Bakker, gospel singer and former wife of evangelist Jim Bakker
**March 8**—Dick Allen, baseball player and singer
**March 9**—Bert "Campy" Campaneris, baseball player (Oakland A's)
**March 9**—John Cale, Welsh musician, composer, and songwriter (The Velvet Underground)
**March 9**—Mark Lindsay, musician (Paul Revere and the Raiders)
**March 11**—Peter Eyre, English actor *(The Remains of the Day)*
**March 12**—Paul Kantner, musician (Jefferson Airplane / Jefferson Starship)
**March 12**—Jimmy "The Toy Cannon" Wynn, baseball player (Houston Astros)
**March 14**—Jerry Jeff Walker, country singer ("Mr. Bojangles")
**March 25**—Aretha Franklin, singer known as the "Queen of Soul" ("Respect," "Think")

Joseph Biden Jr., born on November 20, would be destined to a career in public service, culminating in the vice presidency of the United States.

# Famous People Born in 1942

**March 25**—Jacqueline Lichtenberg, sci-fi author *(Dreamspy)*
**March 25**—Paul Michael Glaser, actor *(Starsky and Hutch)*
**March 25**—Richard O'Brien, English actor and writer *(The Rocky Horror Picture Show)*
**March 27**—Michael York, English actor *(Logan's Run)*
**March 27**—John E. Sulston, English chemist and Nobel Prize winner
**March 28**—Daniel Dennett, philosopher and cognitive scientist
**April 1**—Phil Margo, singer (The Tokens)
**April 1**—Samuel R. Delany Jr., sci-fi author *(Babel-17)*
**April 3**—Wayne Newton, singer ("Danke Schoen")
**April 5**—Allan Clarke, English musician (The Hollies)
**April 12**—Frank Bank, actor *(Leave It to Beaver)*
**April 13**—Bill Conti, film music composer *(For Your Eyes Only, Rocky)*
**April 19**—Alan Price, English musician (The Animals)
**April 19**—Jack Roush, American racing entrepreneur
**April 23**—Sandra Dee, actress *(Gidget)*
**April 24**—Barbra Streisand, award-winning singer and actress ("People")
**April 24**—Richard M. Daley, mayor of Chicago (1989–2011)
**April 26**—Bobby Rydell, rock singer ("Wild One," "Volare")
**April 26**—Claudine Auger, French actress *(Thunderball)*
**April 29**—Klaus Voormann, musician (Manfred Mann), artist, and music producer
**May 1**—Stephen Macht, actor *(Cagney and Lacey)*
**May 4**—Ronnie Bond, musician (The Troggs)
**May 5**—Tammy Wynette, country singer ("Stand by Your Man")
**May 8**—Jim "Motorhead" Sherwood, musician (Mothers of Invention)
**May 9**—John D. Ashcroft, U.S. attorney general (2001–2005)
**May 12**—Ian Dury, musician (Ian Dury and the Blockheads) and actor
**May 17**—Taj Mahal, blues singer and songwriter ("Teacup's Jazzy Blues Tune")
**May 23**—Zalman King, actor and director *(Red Shoe Diaries)*
**May 24**—Derek Quinn, English musician (Freddie and the Dreamers)
**June 1**—Tom Mankiewicz, screenwriter *(Diamonds Are Forever, Superman: The Movie)*
**June 3**—Curtis Mayfield, blues and soul musician ("Freddie's Dead," "Superfly")
**June 15**—Bruce Dal Canton, baseball player (Pittsburgh Pirates)
**June 16**—Eddie Levert, soul singer (The O'Jays)
**June 17**—Mohamed ElBaradei, recipient of the 2005 Nobel Peace Prize
**June 18**—Paul McCartney, English musician and songwriter (The Beatles, Wings)
**June 18**—Roger Ebert, film critic and author
**June 19**—Elaine "Spanky" McFarlane, singer (Spanky and Our Gang)

**June 20**—Brian Wilson, musician (The Beach Boys)
**June 24**—Michele Lee, actress *(The Love Bug)*
**June 24**—Mick Fleetwood, English musician (Fleetwood Mac)
**June 26**—Larry Taylor, musician (Canned Heat)
**July 1**—Andraé Crouch, gospel singer ("The Blood Will Never Lose Its Power")
**July 3**—Kurtwood Smith, actor *(RoboCop)*
**July 10**—Ronnie James Dio, musician (Dio, Black Sabbath)
**July 13**—Harrison Ford, actor *(Star Wars, Raiders of the Lost Ark)*
**July 13**—Roger McGuinn, musician (The Byrds)
**July 17**—Don Kessinger, baseball player (Chicago Cubs)
**July 23**—Madeline Bell, soul singer ("I'm Gonna Make You Love Me")
**July 24**—Chris Sarandon, actor *(Fright Night, The Princess Bride)*
**August 1**—Jerry Garcia, musician (The Grateful Dead)
**August 7**—B.J. Thomas, singer ("Raindrops Keep Falling on My Head")
**August 7**—Gary Edward "Garrison" Keillor, radio personality and creator of *A Prairie Home Companion*
**August 7**—Tobin Bell, actor *(Saw)*
**August 9**—Tommie Agee, baseball player (New York Mets)
**August 11**—Mike Huggs, musician (Manfred Mann)
**August 19**—Fred Thompson, politician and actor *(The Hunt for Red October)*
**August 20**—Isaac Hayes, singer, composer ("Shaft"), and actor
**August 22**—Kathy Lennon, singer (The Lennon Sisters)
**August 23**—Patricia McBride, dancer (New York City Ballet)
**August 25**—Walter Williams, singer (The O'Jays)
**August 27**—Daryl Dragon, musician (The Captain and Tennille)
**September 1**—C.J. Cherryh, Hugo-winning sci-fi author *(Downbelow Station)*
**September 4**—Merald "Bubba" Knight, singer (Gladys Knight and the Pips)
**September 5**—Werner Herzog, director *(Fitzcarraldo, Nosferatu the Vampyre)*
**September 7**—Richard Roundtree, actor *(Shaft)*
**September 15**—Chelsea Quinn Yarbro, sci-fi author *(Hotel Transylvania)*
**September 16**—Bernie Calvert, musician (The Hollies)
**September 21**—Ann Elder, comedienne *(Laugh-In)*
**September 26**—Kent McCord, actor *(Adam-12)*
**September 27**—Alvin Stardust, English singer ("My Coo Ca Choo")
**September 28**—Grant Jackson, baseball player (New York Yankees)
**September 28**—Marshall Bell, actor *(Total Recall)*
**September 29**—Ian McShane, English actor *(Deadwood, Lovejoy)*
**September 29**—Jean-Luc Ponty, French musician and composer *(Enigmatic Ocean)*

## Famous People Born in 1942

**September 29**—Madeline Kahn, actress *(Young Frankenstein, Clue)*
**September 30**—Frankie Lymon, musician (Frankie Lymon and the Teenagers)
**October 3**—Alan Rachins, actor *(L.A. Law)*
**October 6**—Britt Ekland, Swedish actress *(The Wicker Man)*
**October 10**—Peter Coyote, actor *(E.T.: The Extra-Terrestrial)*
**October 12**—Daliah Lavi, singer and actress *(The Silencers)*
**October 12**—Melvin Franklin, singer (The Temptations)
**October 15**—Penny Marshall, actress and director *(Laverne & Shirley)*
**October 18**—Willie Horton, baseball player (Detroit Tigers)
**October 21**—Elvin Bishop, musician ("Fooled Around and Fell in Love")
**October 22**—Annette Funicello, actress *(The Mickey Mouse Club)*
**October 22**—Bobby Fuller, musician ("I Fought the Law")
**October 23**—Michael Crichton, author *(The Andromeda Strain, Jurassic Park)*
**October 26**—Bob Hoskins, English actor *(The Long Good Friday)*
**October 27**—Lee Greenwood, singer ("God Bless the USA")
**October 29**—Bob Ross, artist and television personality *(The Joy of Painting)*
**October 31**—David Ogden Stiers, actor *(M*A*S*H)*
**October 31**—Dave McNally, baseball player (Baltimore Orioles)
**November 1**—Marcia Wallace, actress *(The Bob Newhart Show, The Simpsons)*
**November 2**—Stefanie Powers, actress *(The Girl From U.N.C.L.E., Hart to Hart)*
**November 7**—Johnny Rivers, singer ("Secret Agent Man")
**November 8**—Angel Cordero Jr., thoroughbred horse racing jockey
**November 17**—Bob Gaudio, musician (The Four Seasons)
**November 17**—Martin Scorsese, director *(Taxi Driver, Goodfellas)*
**November 18**—Linda Evans, actress *(Dynasty)*
**November 18**—Susan Sullivan, actress *(Falcon Crest, Castle)*
**November 19**—Calvin Klein, fashion mogul
**November 20**—Joseph R Biden Jr., vice president of the United States (2009–)
**November 24**—Billy Connolly, Scottish comedian and actor *(The Boondock Saints)*
**November 25**—Tracey Walter, actor *(Repo Man, Batman)*
**November 26**—Olivia Cole, Emmy award–winning actress *(Roots)*
**November 27**—Jimi Hendrix, musician ("Purple Haze," "Voodoo Child")
**December 1**—John Crowley, sci-fi author *(Little, Big)*
**December 4**—Gemma Jones, English actress *(Bridget Jones's Diary)*
**December 8**—Bobby Elliott, English musician (The Hollies)
**December 12**—Mike Pinder, English musician (The Moody Blues)
**December 30**—Fred Ward, actor *(The Right Stuff, Remo Williams)*
**December 30**—Michael Nesmith, musician (The Monkees) and actor
**December 31**—Andy Summers, English musician (The Police)

An orange in 1942 would set the buyer back one cent; six pounds of new potatoes, 23 cents.

# The **Cost** of **Living** in 1942

Though the minimum wage in 1942 was about 30 cents an hour, a dollar went a lot further back then—in fact, one dollar then was equivalent to about $13.42 in modern currency. The Emergency Price Control Act of January 1942 gave the government's Office of Price Administration the power to set fixed prices for a wide variety of consumer goods in order to stabilize the economy during the war. Still, they couldn't seem to get a handle on inflation: the September 1942 *Economic Record* of the National Industrial Conference Board asserted that "the annual food bill of the average wage-earner's family was $170 higher at August 1942 prices than at August 1939 prices." Frustrated, in September 1942 FDR introduced sweeping measures for price regulation and appointed former U.S. senator James Byrnes head of the newly created Office of Economic Stabilization, with broad powers to fight inflation, fix prices, and control profits. Alas, as the economist F.A. Hayek rightly pointed out, "the curious task of economics is to demonstrate to men how little they really know about what they imagine they can design." The following month alone, food costs went up 2.5 percent, while the overall cost of living soared higher and higher.

Ration books were used to purchase many items—after all, with a world war raging, even food was a precious commodity. Things like new tires or nylon stockings? Forget about it! With so much raw material channeled into the war effort, people were issued ration books and tokens to get their allotment of everything from gasoline to sugar. By the end of 1942, half of civilian cars displayed an "A" sticker, allowing them four gallons of gas a week. Drivers with other specialized stickers could purchase up to eight gallons a week. Still, shortages persisted, and by early 1943 even staples like cheese and meat were in scarce supply.

A cold bottle of Coca-Cola on a hot day cost a nickel, but the bottle could be returned later for a credit.

## The Cost of Living in 1942

**Statistics about American life in 1942:**
In 1942, the **average house** cost $6,827.
The **average car** cost $920.
The **average wage** was $1,561.
The **average cost of rent** was $35 per month.

**Items rationed in 1942:**
Tires: January 1942 to December 1945
Cars: February 1942 to October 1945
Bicycles: July 1942 to September 1945
Gasoline: May 1942 to August 1945
Fuel oil and kerosene: October 1942 to August 1945
Stoves: December 1942 to August 1945
Rubber footwear: October 1942 to September 1945
Sugar: May 1942 to 1947
Coffee: November 1942 to July 1943
Typewriters: March 1942 to April 1944

**Groceries:**
Bar of soap: 15 cents
Gallon of gas: 15 cents
Bottle of Coca-Cola: 5 cents
Bottle of Pepsi-Cola: 5 cents
Bread: 9 cents per loaf
Milk: 60 cents per gallon
Oranges: 1 cent each
Grapefruits: 5 cents
Potatoes: 6 lbs for 23 cents
Apples: 4 lbs for 25 cents
First-class postage: 3 cents
Movie ticket: 30 cents
Smoked ham: 34 cents per pound
*Life* magazine: 10 cents
Kellogg's Corn Flakes: 8 cents
One 1/4 oz Hershey bar: 5 cents

The 1942 menu from the long-demolished Stacy-Trent Hotel in Trenton, New Jersey, offers a glimpse of restaurant prices of the day:

The average movie theater charged 30 cents a ticket, air conditioning included.

**Appetizers and relishes:**
    Grapefruit: 15 cents
    Fruit cocktail: 25 cents
    Green olives: 15 cents
    Heart of celery: 20 cents
    Celery and olives: 25 cents
    Fresh shrimp cocktail: 45 cents
    Crab meat cocktail: 50 cents
    Tomato juice cocktail: 15 cents
    Clam juice cocktail: 20 cents
    Bread or rolls and butter: 10 cents

**Seafood to order:**
    Cherrystone clams: 35 cents
    Little Neck clams: 35 cents
    Shrimp Newburg: 90 cents
    Fried filet of sole: 75 cents
    Minced clam stew: 45 cents
    Broiled or fried scallops with bacon: 80 cents
    Cream of tomato soup: 15 cents
    Consommé: 15 cents

**Hot dishes to order:**
    Broiled lamb chop, french fried potatoes: 70 cents
    Holsteiner schnitzel O'Brien: 90 cents
    Minute steak, sauté potatoes: $1.75
    Creamed chicken on toast: 80 cents
    Corned beef hash, poached egg: 60 cents
    Ham and eggs with potatoes: 60 cents
    Broiled pork chop, sliced pineapple: 70 cents
    Broiled young chicken on toast: $1.15
    Grilled ham steak, mushrooms: 90 cents
    Creamed chipped beef on toast: 60 cents
    Calves' liver and bacon: 80 cents
    Poached egg on broiled ham, melted cheese: 70 cents

Women become skilled shop technicians at the Douglas Aircraft Company plant, Long Beach, California, which produced the B-17F ("Flying Fortress") heavy bomber, the A-20 ("Havoc") assault bomber, and the C-47 heavy transport plane.

# Day-by-Day Calendar of 1942

The year 1942 was a dark one not only for America but for the world, as the flames of war continued to spread across the globe. The relentless advance of the Japanese forces in the first half of the year left little room for hope for a speedy end to the war in the Pacific, and the seemingly unstoppable Nazi juggernaut seemed to crush all that stood before it. Still, the leaders of the free world met this grim challenge with determination and resolve, pooling their resources to take the first steps toward ending the tyranny of Germany and Japan over the freedom-loving people of the world. And the people proved themselves up to the challenge, resisting in the conquered territories, even in the face of brutal reprisals, as the citizens of the free world created a mighty force to come to their aid.

It was a time of sharp contrasts. Even as horrific atrocities were conceived and executed by the Axis powers, incredible advances in technology took their first baby steps—nuclear power, computers, jet aircraft, even rockets were becoming a reality. Granted, some of these inventions—the V-2 rocket, for instance—were hardly seen as a benefit when they were first employed, but in time, after the hostilities had ended, those creations would be applied to better, more noble uses, as mankind advanced higher and farther, increasing both knowledge and the desire to acquire more of it.

## JANUARY 1

President Franklin D. Roosevelt and British prime minister Winston Churchill issue a declaration, signed by representatives of 26 countries, to create an international postwar peacekeeping organization called "The United Nations."

## JANUARY 2

Japanese forces occupy Manila in the Philippines.

## JANUARY 3

At the Arcadia Conference, Chiang Kai-shek is named commander in chief of Allied forces in China.

## JANUARY 4

The mighty Chicago Bears triumph 35–42 over the All-Star lineup in the 1942 NFL All-Star game.

## JANUARY 5

U.S. mobilization for World War II continues.

## JANUARY 6

The Pan American Airlines *Pacific Clipper* becomes the first commercial airplane to fly around the world.

## JANUARY 7

The three-month-long siege of the Bataan Peninsula begins in the Philippines.

## JANUARY 8

President Roosevelt makes the cover of *Time* magazine this week as their Man of the Year for 1941. He had already been so honored twice before, in 1932 and 1934.

## JANUARY 9

"The Brown Bomber," boxer Joe Louis, defends his world heavyweight championship against Buddy Baer, knocking him out in the first round.

## JANUARY 10

The day after successfully defending his title, Joe Louis enlists as a private in the U.S. Army at Camp Upton, Long Island.

## JANUARY 11

Japanese forces conquer Kuala Lumpur in Malaya.

## JANUARY 12

FDR reestablishes the National War Labor Board for labor dispute settlement and wage stabilization in essential wartime industries.

## JANUARY 13

Henry Ford patents a method of constructing plastic auto bodies 30% lighter than their metal counterparts.

## JANUARY 14

As the Arcadia Conference in Washington, D.C., comes to a close, FDR and Winston Churchill agree to make the defeat of the German war machine their first priority.

## JANUARY 15

President Roosevelt pens the "Green Light" letter, a personal appeal to baseball commissioner Kenesaw Mountain Landis to continue baseball during WWII.

Day-by-Day Calendar of 1942

## JANUARY 16

Auto executive William S. Knudsen becomes the first civilian to join the army at the lofty rank of lieutenant general. His job: consultant and troubleshooter for the war production effort.

President Franklin D. Roosevelt

## JANUARY 17

The U.S. Army deploys men on horseback to locate a TWA Skysleeper that had crashed in flames the previous day with 22 people aboard, including movie siren Carole Lombard; unfortunately, there were no survivors.

## JANUARY 18

The Soviet 54th Army smashes through German defenses at Pogost'e, 25 miles southwest of Leningrad.

## JANUARY 19

The seemingly unstoppable Japanese forces invade Burma.

## JANUARY 20

Nazi officials outside of Berlin hold the Wannsee Conference, in shichthe infamous "final solution" for the complete extermination of Europe's Jews is laid out.

## JANUARY 21

Count Basie records his second version of "One O'Clock Jump."

## JANUARY 22

Japanese forces massacre 110 Australian and 40 Indian wounded and medics at Parit Sulong; after the war, Imperial Guard commander General Takuma Nishimura would be executed for war crimes.

## JANUARY 23

The British Eighth Army liberates Tripoli from Nazi occupation.

## JANUARY 24

The Japanese invasion of the Dutch East Indies begins.

## JANUARY 25

The presidentially appointed Roberts Commission finds the commanders of Pearl Harbor, Adm. Husband Kimmel and Gen. Walter Short, guilty of dereliction of duty for not taking adequate precautions against attack.

## JANUARY 26

The Yanks are coming! The first WWII U.S. forces in Europe go ashore in Northern Ireland.

## JANUARY 27

Winston Churchill faces a vote of no confidence in the House of Commons for his handling of the war; he wins the vote with only one dissenter.

## JANUARY 28

The Glenn Miller Orchestra's recording of "Chattanooga Choo Choo" chugs along in the number one spot; it would hold steady for a total of nine weeks after it topped the charts on December 7, 1941.

## JANUARY 29

Japanese submarines begin harassing British ships along vital trade routes from India.

## JANUARY 30

Adolf Hitler gives his opinion of Winston Churchill in a speech to Nazi loyalists: "This arch-liar today shows that Britain never was in a position to wage war alone. This gabbler, this drunkard Churchill. And then his accomplice in the White House, this mad fool."

## JANUARY 31

Bond girl Daniela Bianchi *(From Russia With Love)* is born in Rome, Italy.

Day-by-Day Calendar of 1942

## FEBRUARY 1

Nazi puppet Vidkun Quisling is named Norwegian premier for the second time; he proceeds to deliver his reappointment speech in German.

British Prime Minister Winston Churchill

## FEBRUARY 2

Daniil Kharms, the Russian surrealist author, dies in a Soviet hospital during the siege of Leningrad.

## FEBRUARY 3

The Japanese stage their first air raid on Java.

## FEBRUARY 4

Brigadier General Clinton Pierce becomes the first U.S. general wounded in action in WWII at Bataan.

## FEBRUARY 5

*Woman of the Year,* starring Katharine Hepburn and Spencer Tracy, opens at Radio City Music Hall. It's the first of nine films starring the famous duo.

## FEBRUARY 6

Bassist John London is born in Texas.

## FEBRUARY 7

Thank goodness for high ceilings! Cornelius Warmerdam pulls off the first indoor 15-foot pole vault.

## FEBRUARY 8

Igor Stravinsky's *Danses Concertantes* premieres in Los Angeles, California.

## FEBRUARY 9

Daylight Savings War Time goes into effect in the United States.

## FEBRUARY 10

Glenn Miller is awarded the very first gold record in recognition of selling one million copies of the hit song "Chattanooga Choo Choo."

## FEBRUARY 11

Archie, the redheaded teen from Riverdale, gets his own comic.

## FEBRUARY 12

Grant Wood, who painted the iconic *American Gothic,* dies at age 49.

## FEBRUARY 13

Adolf Hitler calls off Operation Seelowe—the Nazi invasion of England.

## FEBRUARY 14

The Maastunnel in Rotterdam opens to the public. The unofficial opening ceremony is held in secret to avoid Nazi participation.

## FEBRUARY 15

Singapore surrenders to the Japanese.

## FEBRUARY 16

A small German U-boat attacks ships and an oil refinery on the island of Aruba (a U.S. protectorate at the time), the first shelling of U.S. soil in the war.

Day-by-Day Calendar of 1942

## FEBRUARY 17

Huey Newton, Black Panther leader, is born in Monroe, Louisiana.

Joe Louis, the "Brown Bomber"

### FEBRUARY 18

Japanese troops land on Bali.

### FEBRUARY 19

FDR orders the immediate detention and internment of all "enemy aliens," and West Coast Japanese-American citizens are rounded up and placed in camps for the duration of the war.

### FEBRUARY 20

Lieutenant Edward Henry "Butch" O'Hare singlehandedly shoots down five Japanese heavy bombers, successfully defending the USS *Lexington* and becoming America's first WWII flying ace.

### FEBRUARY 21

Actress-director Margarethe Von Trotta is born in Berlin, Germany.

### FEBRUARY 22

FDR orders General Douglas MacArthur to evacuate the Philippines as American defenses collapse.

## FEBRUARY 23

A long-range Japanese submarine surfaces off the California coast and shells an oil refinery near Santa Barbara, California. It doesn't do much damage to the refinery, but it inflames the fear of invasion.

## FEBRUARY 24

Panic in the streets! Air raid sirens blare over Los Angeles as four antiaircraft batteries open fire on a fleet of invading Japanese airplanes! Or is it?

## FEBRUARY 25

Nope. Turns out that the "Battle of Los Angeles" was fought against a weather balloon—but the hysteria the incident evoked was quite real.

## FEBRUARY 26

Theoretical physicist Werner Heisenberg makes a presentation to Reich officials about a radical idea he and others have been working on: energy acquisition from nuclear fission.

## FEBRUARY 27

English physicist James Stanley Hey discovers radio emissions from the sun.

## FEBRUARY 28

A race riot erupts in Detroit, Michigan, where white residents of the Sojourner Truth Housing Project ironically object to living side by side with black Americans. The confrontation turns violent.

## MARCH 1

The three-day Battle of the Java Sea ends with a major naval defeat for the United States.

## MARCH 2

The 14th annual Academy Awards are held. *How Green Was My Valley*, Gary Cooper, and Joan Fontaine win the top honors.

## MARCH 3

In a Japanese attack on Broome in Western Australia, 88 people are killed.

## MARCH 4

Fool us once, shame on you: Operation K, the Japanese follow-up to Pearl Harbor, meant to disrupt repair and recovery, begins. It is unsuccessful.

## MARCH 5

Dmitri Shostakovich's 7th Symphony premieres in Kuybyshev (now Samara).

## MARCH 6

Glenn Miller continues to dominate U.S. music charts; "Moonlight Cocktail" is number one.

An SBD-2 Dauntless dive bomber prepares for takeoff from the carrier *USS Enterprise* during the February 1, 1942, Marshall Islands Raid.

## 1942: The Year in History

### MARCH 7

Graduation day! The first African-American cadets from the flying school at Tuskegee, Alabama, earn their wings.

### MARCH 8

World champion Cuban chess player José R. Capablanca dies, age 53.

### MARCH 9

Construction of the Alaska Highway begins.

### MARCH 10

Sir William Henry Bragg, winner of the Nobel Prize in physics for his work with x-rays, dies.

### MARCH 11

Grim destination: the first deportation train leaves Paris for the Auschwitz concentration camp.

## MARCH 12

The first American convoy arrives at strategically vital New Caledonia—
15 large ships escorted by a dozen cruisers and destroyers.

## MARCH 13

Julia Flikke, superintendent of the Nurse Corps,
becomes the first woman colonel in U.S. Army.

## MARCH 14

British actress Rita Tushingham *(Doctor Zhivago)* is born.

## MARCH 15

Composer Alexander von Zemlinsky
*(Lyric Symphony)* dies, age 70.

## MARCH 16

A partial solar eclipse takes place.

## MARCH 17

General Douglas MacArthur arrives in Australia
to become supreme commander of the Allied forces.

## MARCH 18

Two African-American baseball players raise eyebrows by requesting a tryout with the Chicago White Sox. Their names: Jackie Robinson and Nate Moreland.

## MARCH 19

FDR orders men between 45 and 64 years old to register for nonmilitary duty.

## MARCH 20

General MacArthur vows, "I shall return" to the Philippines. He does, in 1944.

## MARCH 21

Jimmie Fiedler's column in the *Los Angeles Times* reports that "the war has created a narcotics shortage in Los Angeles, so that many addicts are getting clean and sober or switching to liquor."

## MARCH 22

Sir Stanford Cripps meets with Mohandas Gandhi for the first time. The first item on the agenda: India's defense against the Japanese empire.

## MARCH 23

Historian Samuel Eliot Morison offers his services to FDR as a "sea-going historiographer," recording the exploits of the navy during the war.

*Woman of the Year* was the first of the famed Spencer Tracy / Katharine Hepburn films.

## MARCH 24

The USS *California* is refloated at Pearl Harbor; she would be back in the fight by early 1944.

## MARCH 25

It is announced that 25 of America's best female pilots will go to England to help with the war effort.

## MARCH 26

Erica Jong, author of the novel *Fear of Flying*, is born in New York City.

## MARCH 27

Still the champ! Joe Louis KOs Abe Simon to retain his heavyweight boxing title in New York City.

## MARCH 28

Stanford beats Dartmouth 53–38 for the NCAA men's basketball championship.

## MARCH 29

Lübeck, Germany, is bombed by the Royal Air Force.

## MARCH 30

This week's *Life* magazine features a cover story on the legendary "Flying Tigers."

## MARCH 31

Michael Savage, talk radio host and commentator, is born in the Bronx, New York.

## APRIL 1

Mexico changes from three time zones to two.

## APRIL 2

Actor Roshan Seth *(Indiana Jones and the Temple of Doom)* is born in India.

## APRIL 3

Stuntman Rick Sylvester is born; he would perform the world-record parachute jump for the James Bond film *The Spy Who Loved Me*.

## APRIL 4

Poison-pen biographer Kitty Kelly is born.

## APRIL 5

Welsh director Peter Greenaway *(The Cook, the Thief, His Wife & Her Lover)* is born in Newport, Monmouthshire, Wales.

## APRIL 6

Firesign Theater comedian Phil Austin is born.

## APRIL 7

A heavy German assault on Malta takes place.

Day-by-Day Calendar of 1942

## APRIL 8

The ballet *Pillar of Fire* by Antony Tudor premieres in New York City.

## APRIL 9

The Battle of Bataan continues to go badly: U.S. and Filipino forces are overwhelmed by Japanese attackers.

With so many male workers in the armed forces, women come into their own in the workplace.

### APRIL 10

The Dutch ration cigarettes and candy.

### APRIL 11

Merchant Marines are now authorized to receive the Distinguished Service Medal.

### APRIL 12

Byron Nelson wins the ninth Masters Tournament golf championship.

### APRIL 13

Henk Sneevliet, leader of the Dutch Revolutonary Socialist Party, is executed.

### APRIL 14

A German U-85 is sunk by the USS *Roper* off the coast of North Carolina.

## APRIL 15

King George VI awards the George Cross to the people of Malta.

## APRIL 16

Baseball player Jim Lonborg is born.

## APRIL 17

French general Henri Giraud escapes from his castle prison in Festung Königstein.

## APRIL 18

The *Stars and Stripes* newspaper, directed at the U.S. armed forces, starts publication.

## APRIL 19

Joe Smith wins the 46th Boston Marathon.

## APRIL 20

German occupiers declare
Dutch beaches off limits to civilians.

## APRIL 21

Gospel singer Bobby McClure
("Peak of Love") is born.

## APRIL 22

U.S. forces arrive in India.

## APRIL 23

Allied forces begin bombing Rostock,
Germany; the attack would last four days.

## APRIL 24

Cosmonaut Valeri Abramovich Voloshin is born.

Day-by-Day Calendar of 1942

## APRIL 25

Expressionist author Paul Kornfeld dies.

## APRIL 26

A devastating coal mine explosion kills more than 1,000 people in China.

General Douglas MacArthur

## APRIL 27

A tornado wipes out Pryor, Oklahoma, leaving 100 dead and 300 injured.

## APRIL 28

Put out that light! The nightly "dim-out" begins along the East Coast.

## APRIL 29

Jews are ordered to wear the six-pointed "Jewish star" in the Netherlands and in Vichy-France.

## APRIL 30

The first submarine built on the Great Lakes is launched.

## MAY 1

Radio Orange calls for the oppressed to defy the Nazi order to display the Jewish star.

## MAY 2

At the 68th Kentucky Derby,
Wayne D. Wright rides Shut Out to victory.

## MAY 3

Japanese troops attack the Solomon
Islands, east of Papua New Guinea.

## MAY 4

The Battle of the Coral Sea begins. It is
the first sea battle fought only in the air.

## MAY 5

Sugar rationing begins in the United States.

## MAY 6

Corregidor Island in the Philippines
surrenders to Japanese armies.

## MAY 7

The Battle of the Coral Sea ends
when the Japanese are stopped cold.

## MAY 8

The aircraft carrier USS *Lexington* goes down, sunk
by Japanese during the Battle of the Coral Sea.

## MAY 9

Pop musician Tommy Rowe
("Dizzy") is born in Atlanta.

## MAY 10

Singer Bill Coday is born
in Coldwater, Mississippi.

## MAY 11

Japanese troops conquer Kalewa, Burma.

Day-by-Day Calendar of 1942

## MAY 12

Too close for comfort: a German U-boat sinks an American cargo ship at the mouth of the Mississippi River.

Tuskegee Airmen Colonel Benjamin O. Davis and Edward C. Gleed

## MAY 13

The first cross-country flight
by helicopter takes place.

## MAY 14

The U.S. Women's Army
Auxiliary Corps (WAAC) is formed.

## MAY 15

Gasoline rationing begins in 17
eastern states of the United States.

## MAY 16

The first transport of British and Dutch
prisoners to South Burma takes place.

## MAY 17

The Dutch SS vows loyalty to Adolf Hitler.

## MAY 18

Night baseball games are halted in
New York City for the duration of the war.

## MAY 19

British politician and TV personality
Robert Kilroy-Silk is born.

## MAY 20

The number one song in the country
is "Tangerine," by Jimmy Dorsey.

## MAY 21

Convoy PQ16 leaves England for Russia.

## MAY 22

Mexico declares war
on Germany and Japan.

### MAY 23

Romanian philosopher Gabriel Liiceanu is born.

### MAY 24

Derek Quinn, of Freddie & the Dreamers fame, is born.

### MAY 25

Musician Brian "Blinky" Davison (The Nice) is born.

### MAY 26

In the start of a battle at Bir Hakeim, Libya, Free French forces resist German and Italian attackers.

### MAY 27

African-American navy cook Dorie Miller is awarded the Navy Cross for heroism at Pearl Harbor.

## MAY 28

Stanley B. Prusiner, American scientist and recipient of the 1997 Nobel Prize in Physiology or Medicine, is born in Des Moines, Iowa.

## MAY 29

Bing Crosby records the greatest-selling record of all time: "White Christmas."

The first digital computing device, the Atanasoff-Berry Computer (ABC), was successfully tested at Iowa State College in 1942.

# 1942: The Year in History

## MAY 30

The U.S. aircraft carrier USS *Yorktown* leaves Pearl Harbor; she would be sunk off Midway Atoll on June 4.

## MAY 31

The Luftwaffe bombs Canterbury, England.

## JUNE 1

Chiang Kai-shek, leader of Allied forces in China, appears on the cover of this week's *Time* magazine.

## JUNE 2

Red Sox baseball star Ted Williams enlists as a navy aviator.

## JUNE 3

The Battle of Midway begins between Japanese and American forces. This naval battle would be a crucial encounter in the Pacific campaign.

## JUNE 4

Capitol Records opens for business. In its first decade, the company would count among its stars Johnny Mercer, Peggy Lee, Nat "King" Cole, and Benny Goodman.

## JUNE 5

The United States declares war on Bulgaria, Hungary, and Romania.

## JUNE 6

The world's first nylon parachute jump by a human is performed by the very confident Adeline Gray.

## JUNE 7

The Battle of Midway ends: Admiral Chester Nimitz achieves the first WWII naval defeat of Japan.

## JUNE 8

Bing Cosby records the Christmas hymn "Silent Night."

## JUNE 9

The Nazi order is given to destroy the village of Lidice, Czechoslovakia, purported to be reprisal for the killing of SS officer Reinhard Heydrich on May 24.

## JUNE 10

In the massacre at Lidice, the Gestapo kills 173 men, sends women and children to concentration camps, and burns the village to the ground.

## JUNE 11

The United States and USSR sign a Lend-Lease agreement, contracting the U.S. to supply materiel to the Soviets during WWII.

## JUNE 12

Anne Frank gets a diary as a birthday present in Amsterdam.

## JUNE 13

The first V-2 rocket launch takes place, at Peenemunde, Germany.

## JUNE 14

Anne Frank begins writing the most famous diary in history.

Mohandas Gandhi writing a document at Birla House, Mumbai, August 1942.

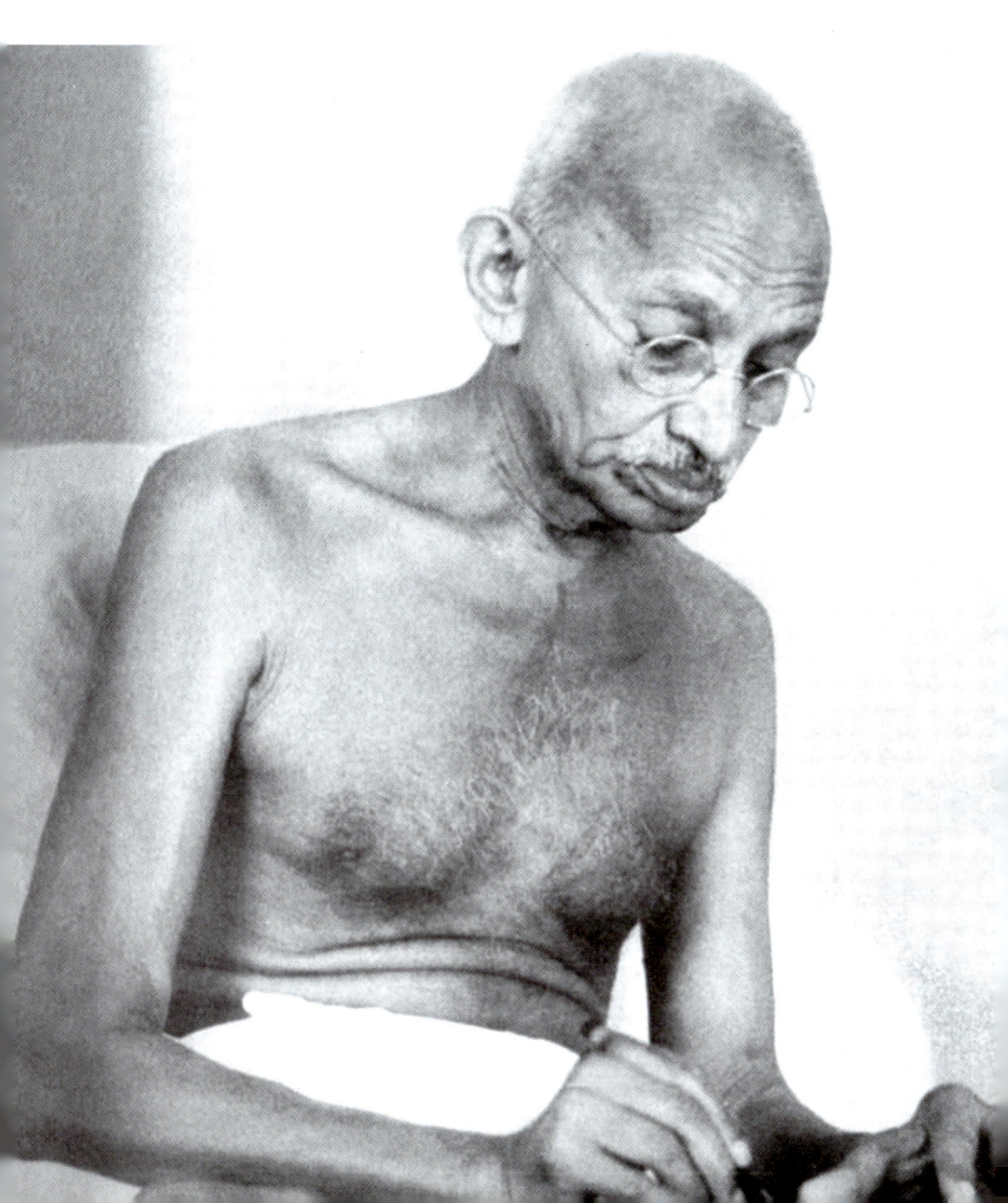

## 1942: The Year in History

### JUNE 15

Rave reviews are published for Walt Disney's *Bambi*, which opened the day before.

### JUNE 16

World motorcycle racing champion Giacomo Agostini is born in Italy.

### JUNE 17

The first WWII American Expeditionary Force lands in Africa on the Gold Coast.

### JUNE 18

Eric Nessler of France stays aloft in a glider for more than 38 hours.

### JUNE 19

Composer-playwright Jeffrey Moss, who would help shape television's beloved *Sesame Street*, is born.

## JUNE 20

Adolf Eichmann orders the deportation of all Dutch Jews.

## JUNE 21

Field Marshal Erwin Rommel of Germany, the "Desert Fox," takes Tobruk in North Africa.

## JUNE 22

Too close for comfort: a Japanese submarine is discovered in the mouth of the Columbia River in Oregon.

## JUNE 23

Germany's newest fighter, a Focke-Wulf FW190, is captured intact when it mistakenly lands at Pembrey airfield in Wales.

## JUNE 24

Rommel's Afrika Corps occupies Egypt.

## 1942: The Year in History

### JUNE 25

General Dwight D. Eisenhower is appointed
commander of U.S. forces in Europe.

### JUNE 26

Germans begin the assault on
British troops at Mersa Matruh in Egypt.

### JUNE 27

The FBI captures eight Nazi saboteurs from
a submarine off New York's Long Island.

### JUNE 28

The Dumont TV network is now
on the air with WABD in New York.

### JUNE 29

Dmitri Shostakovich's 7th Symphony
is performed for the first time.

Day-by-Day Calendar of 1942

## JUNE 30

Oceanographer Robert Ballard is born; he would gain fame by finding the wreckage of the RMS *Titanic* and the USS *Yorktown,* which had been sunk just weeks before his birth in the Battle of Midway.

## JULY 1

German troops conquer Sebastopol, Crimea.

Posters like this one aimed to boost civilian morale in the face of war rationing.

## JULY 2

Vicente Fox, future president of Mexico, is born.

## JULY 3

Mexican TV personality Paco Stanley is born.

## JULY 4

Baseball player Hal Lanier is born.

## JULY 5

Ian Fleming graduates from a training school for spies in Canada; he would go on to create the legendary fictional spy James Bond.

## JULY 6

Anne Frank, age 13, goes into hiding with her family and four others in Amsterdam.

## JULY 7

Heinrich Himmler, overseer of Nazi concentration camps, decides that medical experiments will be carried out on prisoners in Auschwitz.

## JULY 8

Refik Saydam, prime minister of Turkey, dies in office.

## JULY 9

Actress Edy Williams *(Beyond the Valley of the Dolls)* is born.

## JULY 10

The sterilization of all Jewish woman in Ravensbrück Camp is ordered.

## JULY 11

On "Black Saturday," Jews are terrorized by Nazis in Salonika, Greece.

### JULY 12

The number one song in the country is "(I Got Spurs That) Jingle, Jangle, Jingle" by Kay Kyser.

### JULY 13

The Nazis imprison 800 prominent Dutch citizens as hostages.

### JULY 14

Riots against Jews in Amsterdam break out.

### JULY 15

Dutch Jews are singled out for labor camps.

### JULY 16

French police arrest 13,152 Jews in Paris.

Day-by-Day Calendar of 1942

## JULY 17

Flooding in Pennsylvania kills 15 people.

Admiral C.W. Nimitz pins the Navy Cross on Dorie Miller for his heroic actions during the attack on Pearl Harbor.

## JULY 18

The first jet fighter, the Messerschmitt Me 262 Schwalbe, takes flight.

## JULY 19

Dmitri Shostakovich's 7th Symphony premieres in the United States.

## JULY 20

The Women's Army Auxiliary Corps begins basic training at Fort Des Moines, Iowa.

## JULY 21

NBA star Fred Hetzel is born.

## JULY 22

The Nazis decree and immediately implement a massive resettlement program in Poland.

Day-by-Day Calendar of 1942

## JULY 23

Hitler issues Directive 45: occupy Stalingrad.

Bing Crosby

## JULY 24

Irving Berlin's musical *This Is the Army* premieres in New York City.

## JULY 25

German troops occupy Rostov, Russia.

## JULY 26

The Royal Air Force bombs Hamburg, Germany.

## JULY 27

Egyptologist William Matthew Finders Petrie dies.

## JULY 28

Sportscaster Marty Brennaman is born.

## JULY 29

Actor Tony Sirico *(The Sopranos)* is born.

## JULY 30

President Roosevelt signs a bill creating the women's Naval Reserve (WAVES—for "Women Accepted for Volunteer Emergency Service").

## JULY 31

The total of Allied ships sunk this month by U-boats is 96.

## AUGUST 1

A violent clash in Los Angeles, California, leads to the "Sleepy Lagoon Murder."

## AUGUST 2

Canadian musician Garth Hudson (The Band) is born.

**1942: The Year in History**

## AUGUST 3

Arthur MacArthur, son of Gen. Douglas MacArthur, is featured on the cover of *Time* magazine.

## AUGUST 4

The German occupiers order all Dutch homing pigeons killed.

## AUGUST 5

The British government cancels the Munich Agreement, which had ceded the Sudetenland area of Czechoslovakia to German occupation in 1938.

## AUGUST 6

Churchill fires General Claude Auchinleck. Monty, you're up.

## AUGUST 7

The first American offensive in the Pacific in WWII begins at Guadalcanal in the Solomon Islands.

Day-by-Day Calendar of 1942

## AUGUST 8

Six convicted Nazi saboteurs who landed in the United States are executed in Washington, D.C.

## AUGUST 9

Mahatma Gandhi and 50 others are arrested in Bombay after the passing of the Quit India Resolution.

American Douglas SBD-3 Dauntless dive bombers from the USS *Hornet* about to attack the burning Japanese cruiser *Mikuma* for the third time on June 6, 1942.

# 1942: The Year in History

## AUGUST 10

Award-winning fashion designer Betsey Johnson is born.

## AUGUST 11

Field Marshal Montgomery makes his landing on Gibraltar.

## AUGUST 12

Winston Churchill arrives in Moscow for a meeting with Stalin.

## AUGUST 13

The Manhattan Engineer District is established, marking the official start of the Manhattan Project.

## AUGUST 14

Dwight D. Eisenhower is named commander for the invasion of North Africa.

## AUGUST 15

Martial artist Larry Hartsell is born.

## AUGUST 16

Winston Churchill travels to Cairo from Moscow.

## AUGUST 17

The first European bombing run by U.S. forces is undertaken. Target: Rouen, France.

## AUGUST 18

Carlson's Raiders land on Makin in the Gilbert Islands and kill 350 Japanese soldiers.

## AUGUST 19

General Paulus orders the German 6th Army to conquer Stalingrad, Russia. The resulting struggle would be a turning point in the war.

## AUGUST 20

Dim-out regulations are implemented in San Francisco, California.

## AUGUST 21

Alpine hunters plant a German flag on Elbroezgebergte, Kaukasus.

## AUGUST 22

Brazil declares war on Germany, Japan, and Italy.

## AUGUST 23

The Battle of Stalingrad takes place: 600 German planes bomb Stalingrad, killing 40,000.

## AUGUST 24

British novelist Howard Jacobson, winner of the Man Booker Prize, is born.

Day-by-Day Calendar of 1942

## AUGUST 25

The SS begins transporting Jews from Maastricht in the Netherlands.

## AUGUST 26

The Russian counteroffensive against the Nazis begins in Moscow.

Eight Japanese-American women in front of a barber shop in a "war relocation camp."

## AUGUST 27

Cuba declares war on Germany, Japan, and Italy.

## AUGUST 28

In the ninth NFL Chicago College All-Star game, the Chiciago Bears trounce the College All-Stars, 21–0.

## AUGUST 29

Cinematographer James Glennon *(Return of the Jedi)* is born.

## AUGUST 30

Nazi Germany annexes Luxembourg.

## AUGUST 31

The tally of ships sunk this month by U-boats comes to 108.

## SEPTEMBER 1

A federal judge upholds the indefinite detention of Japanese-Americans in the United States.

## SEPTEMBER 2

German troops enter Stalingrad.

## SEPTEMBER 3

Musician Al Jardine (The Beach Boys) is born.

## SEPTEMBER 4

PGA golfer Ray Floyd is born.

## SEPTEMBER 5

British and U.S. forces bomb Le Havre, France, and Bremen, Germany.

## SEPTEMBER 6

In the 56th U.S. women's tennis national championships, Pauline Betz beats A. Louise Brough.

## SEPTEMBER 7

In the 62nd U.S. men's tennis national championships, Frederick Schroeder Jr. beats Frank Parker.

## SEPTEMBER 8

Musician Brian Cole (The Association) is born.

## SEPTEMBER 9

The Japanese drop incendiary bombs on Mount Emily in Oregon.

## SEPTEMBER 10

British troops land on Madagascar.

Day-by-Day Calendar of 1942    85

**SEPTEMBER 11**

Stand-up comedian Tom Dreesen is born.

General Dwight David Eisenhower

## SEPTEMBER 12

Free Poland and Belgium ask Pope Pius XII to condemn Nazi war crimes.

## SEPTEMBER 13

Cubs shortstop Leonard Merullo makes four errors in one inning.

## SEPTEMBER 14

The New York Yankees win their 13th pennant.

## SEPTEMBER 15

The U.S. aircraft carrier *Wasp* is torpedoed at Guadalcanal.

## SEPTEMBER 16

The Japanese attack on Port Moresby, Papua New Guinea, is repelled.

## SEPTEMBER 17

The army appoints Col. Leslie Groves head of the Manhattan Project.

## SEPTEMBER 18

The Canadian Broadcasting Corporation goes on the air.

## SEPTEMBER 19

Glenn Miller's "(I've Got a Gal in) Kalamazoo" is the number one song on the *Billboard* ranking of best-selling retail records.

## SEPTEMBER 20

The National Congress of Racial Equality (CORE) organizes.

## SEPTEMBER 21

One hundred sixteen hostages are executed by Nazis in Paris.

## SEPTEMBER 22

Astronaut and senator William C. Nelson is born.

## SEPTEMBER 23

The Auschwitz concentration camp begins experimental gassing executions.

### SEPTEMBER 24

Singer Gerry Marsden (Gerry & the Pacemakers) is born.

### SEPTEMBER 25

British jazz pianist John Taylor is born.

### SEPTEMBER 26

Actor Kent McCord *(Adam-12)* is born.

### SEPTEMBER 27

Reinhard Heydrich, the "Butcher of Prague," is appointed an SS general.

### SEPTEMBER 28

The Luftwaffe bombs Stalingrad.

### SEPTEMBER 29

Free French leader Charles de Gaulle cancels the Munich Agreement.

Day-by-Day Calendar of 1942

## SEPTEMBER 30

Admiral Nimitz's B-17 manages to find Guadalcanal using a map from *National Geographic*.

The first nuclear reactor was erected in 1942 in the West Stands section of Stagg Field at the University of Chicago.

# 1942: The Year in History

## OCTOBER 1

The first Little Golden Books are published.

## OCTOBER 2

Welcome to the nuclear age: the first self-sustaining nuclear chain reaction is demonstrated in Chicago, Illinois.

## OCTOBER 3

President Roosevelt forms the Office of Economic Stabilization.

## OCTOBER 4

The German assault on the Stalingrad Tractor factory in Volgograd, Russia, begins.

## OCTOBER 5

The St. Louis Cardinals beat the New York Yankees, four games to one, in the 39th World Series.

## OCTOBER 6

The Allied assault on the oil installations of Bula Ceram begins.

## OCTOBER 7

The U.S. and British governments announce the establishment of the United Nations.

## OCTOBER 8

Soviet engineer Sergei Chaplygin dies.

## OCTOBER 9

Australian autonomy is made official with the Statute of Westminster.

## OCTOBER 10

One thousand three hundred Austrian Jews are transported to Theresienstadt concentration camp.

### OCTOBER 11

A sea battle at Cape Esperance, Guadalcanal, begins.

### OCTOBER 12

The U.S. Navy defeats the Japanese at the Battle of Cape Esperance.

### OCTOBER 13

Baseball's Bob Bailey is born.

### OCTOBER 14

A Japanese battleship strikes Henderson Field at Guadalcanal.

### OCTOBER 15

The German 6th Army occupies the Stalingrad Tractor factory, at a cost of 3,000 German lives.

## OCTOBER 16

The National Boxing Association freezes the titles of those serving in the armed services.

## OCTOBER 17

Singer Gary Puckett (Gary PUckett & the Union Gap) is born.

Two U.S. Navy WAVES aircraft mechanics work on a North American SNJ Texan training plane at Naval Auxiliary Air Station Whiting Field, Pensacola, Florida.

## OCTOBER 18

Russian Symbolist painter Mikhail Nesterov dies.

## OCTOBER 19

Attorney, crime novelist, and child welfare advocate Andrew Vachss is born.

## OCTOBER 20

The Durham Manifesto from Fisk University in Nashville, Tennessee, calls for fundamental changes in race relations.

## OCTOBER 21

Australian race car driver Allan Grice is born.

## OCTOBER 22

U.S. generals Clark and Lemnitzer and French general Mast meet secretly in Algeria to arrange the Allied invasion of French North Africa.

## OCTOBER 23

Britain launches a major offensive at El Alamein, Egypt.

## OCTOBER 24

On the second day of the battle at El Alamein, the British infantry attacks.

## OCTOBER 25

Field Marshal Rommel is back in North Africa.

## OCTOBER 26

At the Battle of the Santa Cruz Islands in the Pacific, the USS *South Dakota* shoots down a record 32 enemy planes.

## OCTOBER 27

The U.S. aircraft carrier USS *Hornet* is sunk off the Santa Cruz Islands, a major blow in the battle.

### OCTOBER 28

In Detroit, Michigan, a train crashes into bus, killing 16 and injuring 20.

### OCTOBER 29

Branch Rickey is named president and general manager of the Brooklyn Dodgers.

### OCTOBER 30

The U.S. aircraft carrier USS *Enterprise* reaches Nouméa, New Caledonia, for repairs needed after the Battle of the Santa Cruz Islands.

### OCTOBER 31

The number of ships sunk by U-boats this month reaches 94.

### NOVEMBER 1

Vice-Admiral Andrew Cunningham becomes British commander in chief.

Day-by-Day Calendar of 1942

## NOVEMBER 2

Operation Supercharge, which would bring victory to the Allies in the Battle of El Alamein in Egypt, begins.

## NOVEMBER 3

Despite Hitler's command to stand and fight, Rommel orders the massive retreat of his exhausted and defeated forces from El Alamein.

A young soldier of the armored forces holds and sights his Garand rifle at Fort Knox, Kentucky.

## NOVEMBER 4

Cabaret performer Marcel Barger is killed at Auschwitz.

## NOVEMBER 5

The Nazis carry out a raid on Greek Jews in Paris.

## NOVEMBER 6

Nazis execute 12,000 Minsk ghetto Jews.

## NOVEMBER 7

FDR becomes the first U.S. president to broadcast in a foreign language—French.

## NOVEMBER 8

Mission accomplished? Hitler proclaims the fall of Stalingrad from a Munich beer hall.

## NOVEMBER 9

German occupiers install Erik Scavenius as Danish premier.

## NOVEMBER 10

Philip Barry's play *Without Love* premieres in New York City; the 1945 film adaptation would star Katharine Hepburn and Spencer Tracy.

In Robstown, Texas, at a Farm Security Administration camp for migrant workers, a young boy builds a model airplane while other children look on.

# 1942: The Year in History

## NOVEMBER 11

Germany completes its occupation of France.

## NOVEMBER 12

The Battle of Guadalcanal begins.

## NOVEMBER 13

The minimum draft age is lowered from 21 to 18.

## NOVEMBER 14

The last Vichy-French troops in Algeria surrender.

## NOVEMBER 15

The Heinkel He 219, a night fighter plane used by the Luftwaffe, makes its first flight.

Day-by-Day Calendar of 1942

### NOVEMBER 16

Actress and dancer Donna McKechnie *(Dark Shadows)* is born.

### NOVEMBER 17

Musician Bob Gaudio of the Four Seasons is born.

### NOVEMBER 18

Thornton Wilder's Pulitzer Prize–winning play *The Skin of Our Teeth* premieres in New York City.

### NOVEMBER 19

Russia launches its winter offensive against the Germans along the Don front.

### NOVEMBER 20

The British 8th Army recaptures Benghazi, Libya.

## NOVEMBER 21

Tweety Bird makes his debut in the Warner Bros. cartoon "A Tale of Two Kitties."

## NOVEMBER 22

Hitler orders Rommel's Afrika Corps to fight to the last man.

## NOVEMBER 23

Japan bombs Port Darwin, Australia.

## NOVEMBER 24

German field marshal Erich von Manstein arrives in Starobelsk, Ukraine.

## NOVEMBER 25

The National Organization for Aid to Underground forms.

Day-by-Day Calendar of 1942

## NOVEMBER 26

Here's looking at you, kid: *Casablanca* premiers at the Hollywood Theatre in New York City.

## NOVEMBER 27

The French navy at Toulon scuttles its ships and subs to deny them to the Nazis.

An infantryman at Fort Belvoir, Virginia, prepares to throw "an American pineapple, the kind the Axis finds hard to digest"—in other words, a hand grenade.

## NOVEMBER 28

Nearly 500 die in a fire that destroys the Cocoanut Grove nightclub in Boston.

## NOVEMBER 29

The United States institutes rationing of coffee.

## NOVEMBER 30

In the 30th Canadian Football League Grey Cup, the Toronto Hurricanes defeat the Winnipeg Bombers 8–5.

## DECEMBER 1

Gasoline is rationed in the United States.

## DECEMBER 2

The first controlled nuclear chain reaction occurs at the University of Chicago.

## DECEMBER 3

Swedish composer Wilhelm Peterson-Berger dies, age 75.

## DECEMBER 4

President Roosevelt orders the dismantling of the Works Progress Administration.

## DECEMBER 5

The West Indies chocolate and coffee drop over the Netherlands takes place.

## DECEMBER 6

Queen Wilhelmina announces the formation of the Dutch Commonwealth.

## DECEMBER 7

This date marks the one-year anniversary of the attack on Pearl Harbor.

## 1942: The Year in History

### DECEMBER 8

Frank Sinkwich is the winner of
the eighth Heisman Trophy Award.

### DECEMBER 9

Dick Butkus, sportscaster and NFL
Hall of Fame linebacker, is born.

### DECEMBER 10

Hitler names Anton Mussert
"leader of Netherland people."

### DECEMBER 11

Australian and Dutch guerrilla troops
are evacuated to Timor near Australia.

### DECEMBER 12

An exercise in futility: the Germans begin
an offensive in southwestern Stalingrad.

Day-by-Day Calendar of 1942

## DECEMBER 13

The Washington Redskins defeat the Chicago Bears 14–6.

A young boy looks at a display of toys in a store window at Christmas.

## DECEMBER 14

Child actor Rex Thompson *(The King and I)* is born.

## DECEMBER 15

Massachusetts issues the first U.S. vehicular license plate tags.

## DECEMBER 16

Hitler orders combat against partisans in Russia and the Balkans.

## DECEMBER 17

Allies in London sentence German war criminals.

## DECEMBER 18

The *Charlotte News* in North Carolina reports that a young woman has been arrested in Atlanta for impersonating a WAAC.

## DECEMBER 19

French crime novelist Jean-Patrick Manchette is born.

## DECEMBER 20

The Japanese bomb Calcutta.

## DECEMBER 21

Memphis soul singer Carla Thomas is born.

## DECEMBER 22

Adolf Hitler signs the order to develop the V-2 rocket as a weapon.

## DECEMBER 23

The Allies begin an air attack on Den Helder, the Netherlands.

## 1942: The Year in History

### DECEMBER 24

The first powered flight of the V-1 buzz bomb
takes place in Peenemunde, Germany.

### DECEMBER 25

Russian artillery and tank units send explosive
Christmas presents to the invading Germans at Stalingrad.

### DECEMBER 26

Future governor of California Gray Davis is born.

### DECEMBER 27

In the NFL Pro Bowl, the NFL All-Stars beat Washington 17–14.

### DECEMBER 28

Robert Sullivan becomes the first pilot to fly the Atlantic 100 times.

### DECEMBER 29

Musician Jerry Summers is born.

Day-by-Day Calendar of 1942

## DECEMBER 30

Race car driver Guy Edwards is born in England.

## DECEMBER 31

As of this date, 60 U-boats were sunk in this month.

Boy Scouts in front of the U.S. Capitol displays a "United Nations Fight for Freedom" poster to help the war effort.

The elegant and sophisticated *Casablanca* may have been a top film of 1942, but sideshows at the county fair were still a big part of the cultural landscape.

RUTH THE ACROBAT

# Pop Culture in 1942

In 1942, swing was king, and Glenn Miller was the King of Swing. His great orchestra turned out hit after hit after swingin' big band hit, and Glenn Miller became the first ever musician to sell a million records, with the smash hit "Chattanooga Choo Choo." Of course, there was no shortage of popular big bands: people flocked to the hit music of Benny Goodman, Kay Kyser, Harry James, Tommy Dorsey, and others. Singing acts such as the Andrews Sisters were household names, and a young crooner named Frank Sinatra was just starting to make a name for himself; at his first solo concert in December of 1942, the blue-eyed troubadour nearly caused a riot among starry-eyed bobby-soxers. "Not since the days of Rudolph Valentino," *Time* magazine would remark the next year, "has American womanhood made such unabashed public love to an entertainer."

On the movie scene, heroism and patriotism ruled. The top-grossing film of 1942 was *Mrs. Miniver*, the story of one English family's joys and sorrows during the first few months of World War II. Also popular were films about the heroism of Allied soldiers, like *Desperate Journey*, and unabashedly patriotic films like *Yankee Doodle Dandy*. Perhaps no film better encapsulated these themes than *Casablanca*, surely one of the best-loved films of all time, in which a cynical expatriate American, played by Humphrey Bogart, rediscovers his patriotism and idealism when he is caught up in events much larger than himself.

Even off the set, Hollywood showed its patriotism: actors like Clark Gable, Jimmy Stewart, Tyrone Power, and Eddie Albert enlisted in the armed services, and actresses like Marlene Dietrich, Betty Grable, Ann Sheridan, and Carole Lombard sold war bonds and traveled to entertain the troops.

In 1942, swing dancing was big, and no one in swing was bigger than orchestra leader Glenn Miller.

# Pop Culture in 1942

**The top 20 most popular songs:**
1. "White Christmas," Bing Crosby
2. "Moonlight Cocktail," Glenn Miller
3. "Chattanooga Choo Choo," Glenn Miller
4. "Jingle Jangle Jingle," Kay Kyser
5. "(I've Got a Gal in) Kalamazoo," Glenn Miller
6. "Tangerine," Jimmy Dorsey
7. "Sleepy Lagoon," Harry James
8. "String of Pearls," Glenn Miller
9. "Blues in the Night," Woody Herman
10. "Deep in the Heart of Texas," Alveno Rey
11. "The White Cliffs of Dover," Kay Kyser
12. "Don't Sit Under the Apple Tree," Glenn Miller
13. "The Pennsylvania Polka," The Andrews Sisters
14. "Jersey Bounce," Benny Goodman
15. "American Patrol," Glenn Miller
16. "Strip Polka," Kay Kyser
17. "There Are Such Things," Tommy Dorsey with Frank Sinatra
18. "Don't Sit Under the Apple Tree," The Andrews Sisters
19. "Night and Day," Frank Sinatra
20. "Somebody Else Is Taking My Place," Benny Goodman

**The top 20 highest-grossing films:**
1. *Mrs. Miniver*, Greer Garson and Walter Pidgeon
2. *Desperate Journey*, Errol Flynn and Ronald Reagan
3. *Random Harvest*, Ronald Colman and Greer Garson
4. *Yankee Doodle Dandy*, James Cagney
5. *Gentleman Jim*, Errol Flynn
6. *Springtime in the Rockies*, Betty Grable
7. *Somewhere I'll Find You*, Clark Gable and Lana Turner
8. *This Gun for Hire*, Veronica Lake and Alan Ladd
9. *Reap the Wild Wind*, John Wayne and Paulette Goddard
10. *Footlight Serenade*, Betty Grable and Victor Mature
11. *Road to Morocco*, Bing Crosby, Dorothy Lamour, and Bob Hope
12. *The Pride of the Yankees*, Gary Cooper
13. *I Married a Witch*, Veronica Lake and Fredric March
14. *Song of the Islands*, Betty Grable and Victor Mature
15. *Casablanca*, Humphrey Bogart and Ingrid Bergman
16. *The Glass Key*, Alan Ladd and Veronica Lake

James Cagney, one of cinema's all-time icons, had a top film out in 1942: *Yankee Doodle Dandy*.

# Pop Culture in 1942

**The top 20 highest-grossing films** *(continued)*:
17. *Johnny Eager,* Robert Taylor and Lana Turner
18. *Tortilla Flat,* Spencer Tracy, Hedy Lamarr, and John Garfield
19. *Woman of the Year,* Spencer Tracy and Katharine Hepburn
20. *The Spoilers,* Marlene Dietrich and John Wayne

**Academy Awards:**
Best Picture: *Mrs. Miniver,* Metro-Goldwyn-Mayer
Best Director: William Wyler, *Mrs. Miniver*
Best Actor: James Cagney, *Yankee Doodle Dandy*
Best Actress: Greer Garson, *Mrs. Miniver*
Best Supporting Actor: Van Heflin, *Johnny Eager*
Best Supporting Actress: Teresa Wright, *Mrs. Miniver*
Special Academy Award: *In Which We Serve*

**Bestselling books:**
*And Now Tomorrow*, Rachel Field
*The Song of Bernadette*, Franz Werfel
*Drivin' Woman*, Elizabeth Chevalier
*The Robe*, Lloyd Douglas

**Famous showbiz deaths:**
January 16: Carole Lombard, actress
May 29: John Barrymore, actor
November 5: George M. Cohan, actor, songwriter, entertainer
November 30: Buck Jones, actor

**Interesting inventions of 1942:**
**Duct/duck tape:** Originally, duct tape was designed to seal up ammunition cases in order to keep ammunition dry. The term *duck tape* was coined shortly after it appeared on the scene because of its reliable waterproofing and because it was made from cotton duck fabric.
**Napalm:** Chemists at Harvard University invented the original version of napalm; the powdery substance was meant for use in bombs and flame throwers. Combine it with gasoline, though, and you've got a sticky goop that doesn't come off your target and burns for a really long time.
**The guided missile:** The earliest prototypes of the V-2, the first guided missile, were created in 1936, but in 1942 German scientists developed the final prototype. After a few missteps, the Germans finally got some wartime use out of them in 1944.

# We Can Do It!

The iconic Rosie the Riveter came into being during World War II.

**Atomic power:** Using early discoveries on the creation of plutonium, scientists were able to create the first fission chain reaction on December 2, 1942. From there, it was relatively easy to develop the nuclear reactor in Chicago—and to get started on the Manhattan Project.

**The computer:** It was called the Atanasoff-Berry Computer, or ABC, and the idea was developed in 1937. In 1942, the invention became a reality, with binary arithmetic, dual processors, regenerative memory, and separate functions for computing and memory.

**Nobel prizes of 1942:** Due to the relentless onslaught of World War II, no Nobel prizes were awarded between 1940 and 1942.

# Credits and Acknowledgments

Maurice Cobbs wrote text and selected images. Individual image credits are as follows.

Chapter 1—Muhammad Ali: Ira Rosenberg. Martin Scorsese: David Shankbone. Aretha Franklin: Cecilio Ricardo, U.S. Air Force. Joseph Biden Jr.: Andrew Cutraro, White House photographer.

Chapter 2—Grocery store: John Vachon. Boys drinking Coca-Cola: Library of Congress. Movie theater: John Vachon.

Chapter 3—Female shop technician: Alfred T. Palmer. Franklin D. Roosevelt: Elias Goldensky. Winston Churchill: United Nations Information Office. Joe Louis: Carl Van Vechten. Dive bomber from USS *Enterprise*: U.S. Navy National Museum of Naval Aviation. *Woman of the Year* poster: Metro-Goldwyn-Mayer. Women in the workplace: Alfred T. Palmer. Douglas MacArthur: National Archives. Tuskegee Airmen: Toni Frissell. Atanasoff-Berry Computer: Wikimedia Commons, User:Manop. Gandhi: Anonymous. Rationing poster: Office of War Information. Admiral Nimitz and Dorie Miller: Office of War Information. Bing Crosby: Franklin D. Roosevelt Library. Dive bombers from the USS *Hornet*: U.S. Navy. Japanese-American women: Office of War Information. Dwight David Eisenhower: National Archives. Stagg Field reactor: National Archives. WAVES aircraft mechanics: U.S. Navy. Infantryman with rifle: Alfred T. Palmer. FSA migrant workers' camp: Arthur Rothstein. Infantryman throwing grenade: Office of War Information. Boy and window display: Office of War Information. Boy Scouts: John Rous.

Chapter 4—Ruth the Acrobat: Office of War Information. Glenn Miller: publicity photo. James Cagney: Warner Bros. Studios. Rosie the Riveter: J. Howard Miller for the War Production Co-ordinating Committee.